BIRDS FROM *BRITANNIA*

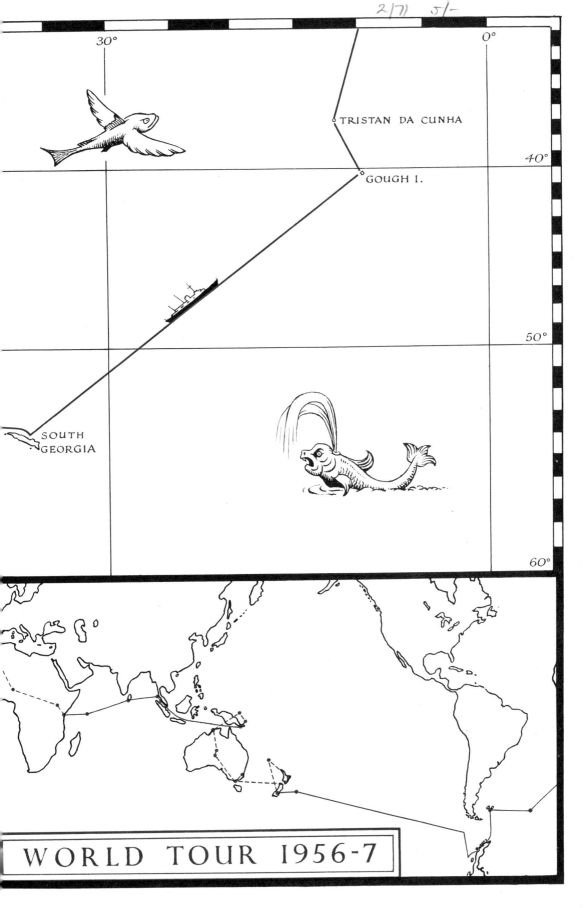

30° 0°

TRISTAN DA CUNHA

40°

GOUGH I.

50°

SOUTH
GEORGIA

60°

WORLD TOUR 1956-7

HIS ROYAL HIGHNESS

The Duke of Edinburgh

BIRDS FROM
Britannia

LONGMANS

LONGMANS, GREEN AND CO LTD
48 GROSVENOR STREET, LONDON WI
RAILWAY CRESCENT, CROYDON, VICTORIA, AUSTRALIA
AUCKLAND, KINGSTON (JAMAICA), LAHORE, NAIROBI
LONGMANS SOUTHERN AFRICA (PTY) LTD
THIBAULT HOUSE, THIBAULT SQUARE, CAPE TOWN
JOHANNESBURG, SALISBURY
LONGMANS OF NIGERIA LTD
W. R. INDUSTRIAL ESTATE, IKEJA
LONGMANS OF GHANA LTD
INDUSTRIAL ESTATE, RING ROAD SOUTH, ACCRA
LONGMANS GREEN (FAR EAST) LTD
443 LOCKHART ROAD, HONG KONG
LONGMANS OF MALAYA LTD
44 JALAN AMPANG, KUALA LUMPUR
ORIENT LONGMANS LTD
CALCUTTA, BOMBAY, MADRAS
DELHI, HYDERABAD, DACCA
LONGMANS CANADA LTD
137 BOND STREET, TORONTO 2

First published 1962

Made and Printed in Great Britain by
Jarrold & Sons Ltd, Norwich

Contents

The illustrations will be found between pp. 46 and 47,
pp. 50 and 51, pp. 58 and 59

Endpaper maps show World Tours
1956-7 and 1959

Introduction

IT all started with the 1956 Olympic Games in Melbourne and the Commonwealth Trans-Antarctic Expedition. I had already agreed to go to the Games when I heard about the plans for the Trans-Antarctic Expedition from Sir Vivian Fuchs. He was to start from the Weddel Sea, and Sir Edmund Hillary was to begin his trek from the Ross Sea. Sir Edmund was due to leave Christchurch in New Zealand in December, not long after the end of the Games. I had visions of visiting both ends of the expedition but they soon faded. However, in discussing these ideas and looking at charts and maps, it soon became obvious that there were a good many island communities and outposts in the Indian Ocean, the South Pacific, Antarctic and Atlantic which cannot be visited by air and which are too remote and too small to get into the more usual tours. Although it meant being away from home for three months, including Christmas and New Year, I decided to try to arrange the journey out to Australia and back by sea in the Royal Yacht *Britannia*.

For various reasons the outward journey began by air to Mombasa in Kenya, where I joined the Yacht on 16 October. Our first call was at the Seychelles Islands in the Indian Ocean; not flat coral reefs but great jutting peaks rising blue-green out of a brilliant sparkling blue sea. Archbishop Makarios was undergoing a period of compulsory retirement there at the time. I didn't meet him then, but when five years later he came to Buckingham Palace with the other Commonwealth Prime Ministers, he reminded me of the visit and told me that he had watched some of the proceedings from his house.

On to Ceylon and then Malaya. I had intended to visit Singapore, but while we were in Ceylon riots broke out in the Chinese schools in Singapore and I was advised to avoid the place. On the passage across we cooked up an entirely new programme for a visit to Malaya instead.

After short visits to Australian-administered Papua and New Guinea, and calling at Darwin and Alice Springs, I flew to Melbourne for the Games.

On 11 December I flew to New Zealand. I also managed a quick excursion to Norfolk Island, north of New Zealand, where some of the descendants of the *Bounty* mutineers were resettled a hundred years ago. It was in the harbour at Christchurch that we met up with Sir Edmund Hillary's party which was about to sail in H.M.N.Z.S. *Endeavour* for the Antarctic and his epic journey to meet Sir Vivian Fuchs at the South Pole. At one time I had hoped to take *Britannia* into the Ross Sea, but I didn't think the risk of being iced up for nine months was worth it.

From New Zealand we sailed for the Chatham Islands. Three hundred miles east of Christchurch, not unlike the Shetlands, rolling, windswept, grassy hills, the only trees stunted and bent by the wind. We attended a race-meeting there and an outdoor Maori cook-up for the whole population. Huge pieces of beef and mutton, cabbages and potatoes were cooked in a large pit in the ground, covered with a sheet and the earth heaped over the top. A most effective way of cooking for a large number of people, and the results were certainly eatable, though I can't imagine the comments of a French chef.

We sailed on 19 December and promptly crossed the date-line and had 19 December all over again, and Commander Adams, the Commander of *Britannia*, had two birthdays.

From the Chatham Islands to the Graham Land Peninsula of the Antarctic continent is 3,800 miles of open sea in the Roaring Forties. As we set off one member of our party was heard to say that if we didn't make it there would be plenty of people to say 'I told you so!' It's strange to think that Magellan, after battling his way through the Straits named after him, emerged into the great ocean which he called *El Mare Pacifico* because of the glorious weather which greeted him; it must have been one of the very rare fine spells in those latitudes.

The old windjammers used the route across the South Pacific from Australia round Cape Horn to England. They crashed across, driven by a succession of westerly gales before rounding Cape Horn and catching the trade winds of the South Atlantic. The passage took us thirteen days, and by a stroke of luck we picked a gap between two gales and crossed in relative comfort. We soon got used to the long heaving swell, but our only company were the seabirds of the southern oceans.

Up to that moment I don't think I had ever deliberately taken a photograph of a bird in my life. My ignorance of birds was sublime; if pressed, I would have admitted that apart from the more obvious game-birds the others came in three categories: sparrows, seagulls and ducks. It was that long passage across the southern Pacific which started me looking at birds, trying to recognize them and photograph them.

In this respect the passage was most rewarding because I noted that we saw the following birds: Sooty, Wandering, Black-browed, Buller and Shy Albatrosses; Grey-faced, White-headed, Antarctic and White-bellied Storm Petrels; a Grey-headed Mollymawk, a flock of prions, a Silver-grey Fulmar and a Sooty Shearwater. Needless to say, not one of the photographs I took on that leg of the journey is printable. My first success was with the Pintado Petrels or Cape Pigeons off the wild coast of the South Shetlands, 460 miles south of Cape Horn. These delightful little petrels swung endlessly to and fro across the stern in flocks of about thirty or forty against a backdrop of great hunks of black and white mountains rearing out of the sea and disappearing into low grey cloud. They were close enough to get good pictures, but they go very fast and it becomes a real problem to keep them in focus long enough to release the shutter.

There is a dark room in the Yacht, so that I could see the results within quite a short time. I did not develop and print pictures myself, largely because, like kitchens, I don't believe it is humanly possible to share a dark room and remain on good terms with the other user.

The Falkland Islands, South Georgia, Gough Island and Ascension Island all provided marvellous opportunities for taking pictures of birds, and the whole journey was over only too quickly as we arrived in Gibraltar on 6 February. A few days later we sailed for Setubal, where the Queen flew out to join the Yacht for a State visit to Portugal.

Three years later, in 1959, I agreed to represent the British Association for the Advancement of Science at the meetings of the Indian Science Congress in Delhi and the Pakistan Association for the Advancement of Science in Karachi. I spent a month travelling about the two countries and then joined the Yacht at Rangoon.

The first journey had taken me to the Antarctic and South Atlantic islands; this time I had arranged to visit Singapore—missed in 1956—Hong Kong, Borneo, the Solomon and Central Pacific Islands. Then through the Panama Canal to Nassau in the Bahamas and finally to Bermuda for their celebrations to mark the 350th anniversary of the island as a Crown colony.

There were fewer opportunities to take photographs of birds on this journey, largely because almost all the islands were inhabited and every minute of the time ashore was worked into the programme. Christmas Island was the most rewarding place and I managed to spend one Sunday afternoon on a small island in the middle of the main lagoon, and most of the pictures of birds of the tropical seas were taken there.

All the photographs in this book were taken during those two journeys, either during the long sea passages, on uninhabited islands, or during an odd afternoon off. It was only on those occasions that I could use a camera at all. As you can imagine, it is not really possible for me to take photographs of any kind, least of all of birds, during a series of official functions even on a Pacific island. There are always plenty of people about with cameras on these occasions, and there are times when I feel full of sympathy for that pair of ospreys which nested in Scotland recently.

I have taken photographs in a vague sort of way for years, punctuated by bouts of enthusiasm and neglect. It must have been during a bout of enthusiasm and extravagance that I bought a Swedish Hasselblad camera in Stockholm. There is no doubt in my own mind that this particular camera has the ability to make what would otherwise be very ordinary pictures look passably good. In the same fit of extravagance I bought a 250 mm. lens, and this combination took most of the photographs in this book. The exceptions are those in which I appear and numbers 51, 52, 53, 54, 56, 58, 59, 60, 61, 62, 63 and 66, which I took with a Minox miniature camera.

Needless to say, it never occurred to me at the time that the photographs might ever be published. If I had thought of it I would have taken a lot more trouble and many more photographs. However, one day I happened to show them to a friend of mine, who knows about birds, and he seemed to think that many of the birds I had taken are not photographed very often, and that therefore the pictures might interest people who like birds.

This is by no means a scientific ornithological book, and it is far from being a comprehensive collection of all the varieties that inhabit the areas through which we travelled. I merely took pictures of whatever birds offered themselves wherever it happened to be convenient. The only merit is that the birds are shown in their natural surroundings. It is in fact completely amateur.

The photographs are in black and white simply because I prefer taking photographs in black and white. Fortunately most of the birds themselves are black and white, or grey anyway. So not much is lost, but to make recognition easier I asked Commander A. M. Hughes, O.B.E., R.N. (RETD.), to produce some detailed illustrations of most of the birds contained in the book. I also asked Captain G. S. Tuck, D.S.O., R.N. (RETD.), Chairman of the Royal Naval Bird Watching Society, to write some general notes about the different birds and their habits because I don't know enough about them, and however good the photograph, it is always nice to know something about the subject.

As this is a book about birds and not about my journeys, the photographs have been grouped according to the areas in which the birds were photographed. This confuses the sequence of the journeys, but it makes greater ornithological sense. The sequence of the sections is southwards, starting with the tropical seas, then the southern oceans and finally the sub-Antarctic and Antarctic. As many of the places are not very well known, there are maps showing the routes of the two journeys inside the front and back covers.

Many people helped to put this book together, and I want to thank Commander Hughes and Captain Tuck for all the trouble they have taken, Longmans for their patience, and in particular Aubrey Buxton for his expert help and advice at all times.

SECTION ONE

The Tropical Seas

I ONLY managed to take photographs of birds belonging to the tropical seas at Christmas Island in the Pacific or in the vicinity of Ascension Island in the South Atlantic.

Ascension Island looks exactly like a huge heap of different coloured cinders or clinkers with a white sandy beach round the edge where turtles lay their eggs. The clinkers vary from bright red, orange and yellow to black. The only bit of green on the island is a tuft on the very top of the central 3,000-foot peak. It is, in fact, the farm for the island which is an important Cable and Wireless station and an American satellite tracking post. There are no permanent inhabitants, but the Cable and Wireless people seem to have made themselves very comfortable in the old naval buildings. There was a naval garrison there from 1810 till 1914. Vast numbers of Sooty Terns, or Wideawakes, nest there. Otherwise the island supports some wild donkeys and sheep.

The church, which was built in the early days of the naval occupation, had many tablets put up to Royal Marines who appeared to form the bulk of the casualties. But there was one rather pathetic little memorial to a young seaman who lost his life while driving the daily cart up Green Mountain. It must have been quite an undertaking in those days because some of our party who went up found it hard enough by car.

The air round the island was full of different kinds of Booby, Frigate Birds and Man-o'-war Birds, and although many of them came quite close there is nothing quite so frustrating as trying to photograph birds in the air. The Hasselblad is a reflex camera, which means that you look through the lens at the subject which is reflected by a mirror on to a ground-glass screen. In order to focus you have to twiddle the whole lens, and then when the button is pressed the mirror folds away and the shutter does its stuff. If the lens is stopped down it is like trying to focus on something on a dark night. If the lens is opened right out, in order to let in more light, there is never time to stop it down again after getting the bird in focus. Luckily it is just as well to use a fast shutter speed and an open lens, because the bird may be flapping its wings.

The next problem is to choose a bird, assuming, that is, that there are more than one about. If you choose the nearest one, it is invariably miles away by the time you have got the camera on to it, and it is obviously not coming back again. If, on the other hand, you choose a bird that looks as if it is coming towards you, it either changes its mind, or it flies about just a bit farther away than you would like until you have taken its picture, whereupon it promptly flies past within six feet.

There is an added hazard which all people with reflex cameras will readily recognize, and that is the distressing tendency to swing the camera the wrong way. This can be overcome with great self-control and much practice, but I never quite got over this difficulty.

The Hasselblad also has some very particular tricks of its own. It is true you can't take a photograph with the lens cover on, but you can attempt to take a photograph without removing the slide which covers the front of the removable film case. The button will not press, and by the time you have taken the slide out you have got to start the whole process again.

At Christmas Island the problems were rather different. Some of the birds were stationary in trees or on the beach. The closer you can get obviously the better, but just how close can you get? The business becomes a kind of 'grandmother's footsteps', one pace too close and the bird flies off. After some trial and error it is possible to judge how close you can get to a certain kind of bird, but only if the bird co-operates by coming back again to its bush or beach when you retire to try again.

Christmas Island was discovered by Captain Cook on Christmas Day, 1777. One of the Line Group, it lies in a dry belt of the Pacific, 1,200 miles south of Hawaii. On most maps it is marked as British, but in fact this claim is disputed by the Americans.

Christmas is rather bigger than the average Pacific island, being almost thirty miles long and twelve miles across, shaped like a frying-pan. Owing to the lack of rainfall it remained uninhabited and much of it is covered with scrubby bushes or entirely barren. One part of it supports some rather unhealthy looking coco-nut palms, and there is now a small community of Gilbert Islanders who are engaged to work on the plantation for periods of a year (married) or eighteen months (single). The work consists of gathering the coco-nuts, splitting them open and scooping the flesh out to be dried in the sun. These pieces of dried nut, called copra, are then bagged and collected for processing into oil in factories all over the world. All the smaller Pacific islands are utterly dependent upon the sale of copra for their income, simply because virtually nothing else will grow on that coral soil.

These islands are roughly circular with a great lagoon in the middle. Sometimes the ring is closed with the central lagoon cut off from the sea, in others the ring is made up of a string of small islands, some connected at low water and others cut off by deep-water channels.

The outsides of the islands are protected from the constant pounding of the long Pacific breakers by coral reefs, some close inshore, others stretching several hundred yards out to sea. The sea is a particular pale blue and over the white coral sand it becomes quite transparent. From the air, boats look as if they are suspended above the ground in some mysterious way as their shadows appear quite separate on the sea floor.

The colour of the sea can vary enormously. The North Sea, for instance, has a peculiar greyish-green colour even in fine weather. The sea off the west of Scotland has a special black look about it, although in the sun it produces the most glorious aquamarines and amethysts. The wine-dark seas of Homer's Mediterranean are again different from the inky black of the Antarctic and to the much greener blue of the Indian Ocean. The long spume-streaked rollers of the North Atlantic and the generally grey climate that goes with them is quite different from the gigantic swell of the South Pacific with its very clear atmosphere and garishly streaked sky of brilliant ochres and purples.

Christmas has a certain gloomy notoriety as the base for testing British atomic weapons. There was much activity at this very interesting base when I was there but no testing. The bird life on the little sandy island in the lagoon continued apparently undisturbed.

The moment we stepped ashore the air filled with wheeling, circling, screeching birds and every tussock hid a shearwater with an egg or young, and every bush held noddies, little Blue-grey Petrels and White Terns. Crested Terns stood serenely on the beach.

I arrived weighed down with cameras and lenses, spare films and goodness knows what else; and it was hot. We didn't have much time, so I was soon in a frenzy about which birds to start on, flying or stationary, whether to use still or ciné, colour or black and white. Oddly enough, the black and white were far the most successful, and for once I could get the birds in focus before they flew off. Almost all of them seemed remarkably unafraid, except for the Crested Terns, which would not let me get closer than about fifty feet.

The little White Terns are charming creatures but maddening to photograph. They appeared to be very interested in the camera and would come and hover about eight feet above my head, peering down at me. This was too good to miss, but I never seemed to be able to wind the focus down from thirty feet to eight feet before they flew off again. However, I noticed that they like to leave a certain branch, fly round and return to it over and over again. This explains the three pictures of the White Tern.

The two pictures of the female Frigate-Bird perched on a bush are a good example of the 'grandmother's footsteps' approach. Peering through the view-finder you walk cautiously towards the bird, keeping it in focus and with one finger on the button. This would be more easily done with three hands, but it is just possible with two. My technique was then to take a picture as soon as the subject was reasonably recognizable and then to move in until the bird got restless; stop, take another one, and then if possible move in and take another as the bird flew off. One of the dis-advantages of this system is that you can't see where you are treading as you advance, with obvious results. In the case of the Frigate Bird she did not come back again, and those were the only photographs I got of her. I don't remember seeing a male and I certainly never saw one with its great red pouch blown up under its beak.

The little land crabs seemed to live in holes at the top edge of the beach. They are quite small, not more than six inches from toe to toe, and they scuttled along just in front of me as I stalked the Crested Terns. If chased, they disappeared into a hole or made for the water at high speed, and dug themselves into the sand.

While I was stalking and snapping I noticed that the five Gilbertese boatmen who had brought us to the island were engaged in catching fish in a net. Judging by the shrieks and splashes, it sounded as if they were really enjoying themselves. As I was only wearing bathing trunks I went and joined them. We walked in line parallel to the shore, about waist-deep until someone spotted a shoal of very pale silvery fish. The procedure was then to run out the net to seaward of the shoal and for those not actually holding the net to jump about and splash in an effort to keep the fish between the net and the shore. A great many got away despite our noisiest efforts, but by the time the net was hauled on to the beach we had usually captured between ten and twenty very active bright shiny white fish of about one pound each. We repeated this berserk manœuvre several times until we had filled two sacks. I've no idea what sort of fish they were and I've forgotten what the Gilbertese called them, but they made very good eating when we got some of them back to the Yacht.

The Gilbert Islanders working on the plantation come from a group of islands on the Equator between the 170th and 180th meridian. They are grouped with the Ellice Islands, about 500 miles to the south, for administration.

The Gilbert and Ellice Islands Colony covers a sea area of 2,000,000 square miles with a total land area of 370 square miles. The population is about 48,000, of whom some 36,000 are Micronesians and 6,000 Polynesians. Generally speaking, the Gilbertese are Micronesians and the Ellice Islanders Polynesians. In looks there is no very marked difference except that the Polynesians are lighter in colour. In character the Ellice Islanders are gayer and more light-hearted, whereas the Gilbertese tend to be rather more serious and independent. The people of both groups, however, are charming, cheerful and civilized, with a great delight in singing and dancing. At each island I was invited to the *Maneaba* or village hall and entertained to a series of ear-splitting songs called *Batere*. Oddly enough it was the Gilbertese expatriates on Christmas who provided the best *Batere* of all. (Perhaps not so oddly—St Patrick's Day, for instance, is frequently observed with greater fervour outside Ireland.)

In the *Maneaba* two groups of men and women squat down at each end of the long, low, open-sided building. Each group surrounds a low plat-form which is thumped by those sitting round it as accompaniment, the others make hand and arm gestures or clap. The songs usually start quietly enough with arms and hands illustrating the words; gradually the tempo and the volume increase and with them the sense of excitement till they end with a great shout. The two groups take it in turns to sing and there is a cheerful rivalry.

One of the songs sounded vaguely familiar, and then it suddenly dawned on us that it was the Gilbertese version of 'Tipperary'. The words were still just recognizable as English, but none of the singers understood what they were singing. I imagine it is quite easily explained, but it came as a great surprise to me.

Owing to the fact that the islands of the two groups are differently shaped, their boats are quite different. The Gilberts have large lagoons open at some point to the sea, but the water inside is reasonably sheltered.

These islanders have developed very fast-sailing outrigger canoes made of planks fastened together. These are used inside the lagoons, and only very occasionally when the weather is suitable will they venture any distance into the open sea. In the Ellice Islands, on the other hand, the lagoons are usually completely enclosed by the atoll and are rather smaller. This means that all the fishing and communication with other islands is over the open sea, with the result that they have developed very sturdy dug-out outrigger canoes propelled by paddles.

I was fortunate enough to go for a sail in one of the Gilbert canoes in the lagoon at Tarawa. It must have been about thirty feet long, but at no point was the beam greater than eighteen inches. The outrigger was a solid spar not quite as long as the canoe, suspended about fifteen feet from the side of the canoe by a number of struts and braces. It had one large lug-sail and it was steered by a long oar. There was a crew of four or five and the thing went extremely fast, throwing up clouds of spray. The art consists of keeping the canoe upright and this is achieved by two or three members of the crew climbing out towards the outrigger as it is lifted out of the water in a puff, and then back towards the canoe as the outrigger drops back in the water again. This needs very careful timing; if they get too far out they are in danger of being swept into the sea; if they don't go far enough the canoe goes over. At times we must have been doing well over fifteen knots.

As the outrigger is on one side of the canoe it always has to be on the windward side, which means that it is impossible to go about in the ordinary way by bringing the wind on to the other bow. In this contrap- tion you have to sail it in the opposite direction, which means shifting the sail and the steering oar from one end to the other; quite a lengthy process. I had a go at steering the canoe, but soon realized that the steering oar had very little effect and that the direction was controlled almost entirely by the trim of the sail.

At Vaitupu in the Ellice Islands I went ashore in one of their dug-out outrigger canoes. The crew consisted of four or five paddlers, singing fit to bust and they kept time by beating their paddles across the top of the canoe. We negotiated the surf over the coral reef very skilfully and then instead of that rather undignified jump on to wet sand, the reception party simply picked up the canoe bodily and carried it, everyone singing, high on to the beach. In the evening I took part in a sortie after flying-fish. These fish come in close to the coral reef in the evenings and the canoes go out, about six or seven of them, take up a crescent formation facing the beach, and drive the fish towards it. When the fish get close to the shore they try to fly out to sea again. At this moment each boat produces two large circular nets on long poles and the fish are caught in the air like butterflies. My attempts with the net were sadly misdirected; in fact I still don't understand how they managed to do it.

Many of the Central Pacific Islands saw some of the bloodiest battles of the campaign in the Pacific during the Second World War. At Tarawa I walked down on to the coral foreshore just outside the Administrator's house and picked up an old rifle cartridge case already whitened by coral growth. Before going another ten yards I could have collected a bucketful. Most of the big stuff has been removed, but the mass of empty small-arms cases which I saw in that short walk was a grim reminder of the fury of the fighting in those parts.

In the battle for Tarawa alone over 1,000 Americans and 4,000 Japanese were killed in four days' fighting. Apart from the empty cartridge cases there are still a few traces of the war, including rusty landing-craft and a burnt-out tank on the beach, Japanese gun emplacements and concrete bunkers. One of the coast defence guns had been part of the British defences at Singapore before being moved to Tarawa, where it was found to be facing the wrong way for the second time.

In the Solomon Islands there are also many reminders of the bitter war: scarred coco-nut trees, twisted wrecks high up on the coral shore, and remains of gun emplacements.

The remarkable thing about it is that even though most of the native people were involved in the fighting and performed wonderful feats of gallantry and loyalty, the whole ghastly episode seems to have left no serious impression upon the life of these lovely peaceful islands. What must they think of the administrators we send out to them, who stop them fighting with bows and arrows and preach law and order, but whose own people seem to think it is perfectly all right to fight each other and involve everyone else with the most destructive weapons science can invent?

Almost all the Central Pacific Islands are low-lying coral atolls, but there are two rather special islands which are quite different. Ocean and Nauru were both pushed up out of the sea by volcanic action, and trapped in the coral rock are huge deposits of phosphate. This is being dug out and processed jointly by Australia, New Zealand and Britain, and in fact almost all the superphosphate used in Australian and New Zealand agriculture comes from these two islands.

I was very sorry to leave the Gilbert and Ellice Islands, and I shall always remember the cheerfulness and natural dignity and good manners of the islanders who are so delightfully described in Arthur Grimble's *A Pattern of Islands*.

SECTION TWO

The Southern Oceans

THERE is no line of demarcation between the tropical seas and the southern oceans, the two gradually merge into each other as the temperature drops.

For convenience I have taken the area of the southern oceans to lie between St Helena, 15° south, and the Falkland Islands, 55° south in the South Atlantic. Strictly speaking, it is a belt the whole way round the southern hemisphere between the Tropic of Capricorn and the Antarctic continent.

We passed through this area on the way across the South Pacific and then from south to north, calling at the Falklands, Gough, Tristan da Cunha and St Helena. However, the ornithological progress of this book is from north to south, so from the tropical island of Ascension we drop down to St Helena.

St Helena is more or less the northern limit of the southern ocean, and it is in fact a strange mixture of tropical and temperate. Unfortunately there was no opportunity to take photographs, and I am sorry to say that I don't remember seeing any birds there, although in several places I could visualize pheasants flying really well.

The coast is steep and barren and it is only after getting inland that the very considerable charm of the island is unfolded.

Jamestown runs up a steep gully and at one point there is a stairway of 699 steps up to the plateau above the town. The boys have a particular technique for sliding down the bannisters: the round trip up the steps and down the bannisters takes about five minutes, but it needs a high standard of fitness.

St Helena has always been intimately involved in the maritime history of the South Atlantic as a provider of fresh provisions for ships in the area. The East India Company maintained farms and gardens for their ships, and during the suppression of the slave trade it became an important depot for the release and repatriation of many African slaves.

This was the cause of the collapse of most of the buildings in Jamestown.

A captured slaver lay off the harbour, abandoned, so before long her timbers found their way ashore. With them came the white ants or termites and within a very short time they had made a meal of every piece of building timber in the island.

Longwood, where Napoleon lived out the last years of his life, was almost entirely destroyed and it was as a virtual ruin that King George VI and Queen Elizabeth saw it on their way home from South Africa in 1947. Queen Elizabeth mentioned the state of the house to the French Ambassador in London, and by the time I went there ten years later the French Government had done an excellent job of restoration. All the woodwork has been renewed, and the rooms redecorated, keeping strictly to the original designs. The walls outside are pink, and both the house and garden are most attractive.

Napoleon's guards were camped on a hill opposite the house so that he could be kept under constant surveillance. He got round this by digging trenches for the paths in the garden and by cutting peepholes in the shutters of his little garden hut. In this way he could enjoy his garden and the view without being seen.

Napoleon spent the first fifty days of his time on the island in The Briars, a house belonging to the Balcombe family. Strangely enough the Duke of Wellington, as Sir Arthur Wellesley, also stayed in that house in 1810 on his way home from India. Part of the house still stands.

Quite close to Longwood in a grove of wild olives lies the grave in which Napoleon was buried before his body was taken to Les Invalides in Paris in 1840. At the time of his death, the English insisted that nothing more than 'General Bonaparte' was to be inscribed on the tomb. Rather than give in, the French put nothing on it at all. The great black slab still lies there without so much as a date on it.

There is hardly any level ground on the island anywhere, and the whole place is cut up by violently steep green hills and valleys. Jacaranda and hibiscus, bougainvillaea and blackberries grow everywhere, and the climate up in the middle of the island seemed very pleasant.

Flax is the main crop, but the outlook is not very good. There are hopes that coffee-growing may be successful as the demand for flax steadily drops. The big countries of the world may have more complicated economic problems, but they are no more urgent than the problems of small islands like St Helena.

Southwards from St Helena albatrosses began to join the ship, first at intervals and later they provided an almost continuous escort. Providing the wind is right the Wandering Albatross is certainly the easiest bird to photograph flying. For one thing it is big—the wing-span can reach fourteen feet but averages about ten—for another it glides relatively slowly and it doesn't mind coming close to the ship. I suppose the nearest I ever saw one was about eight feet away as it sailed slowly past, eyeing me rather haughtily.

It was quite impossible to judge whether one particular bird stayed with us for any length of time because some days we only had one in sight and other days there might be anything up to twenty wheeling and circling. Their flight pattern depended entirely upon the wind relative to the ship. With a head wind or a following wind they would swing to and fro across the stern, sometimes close, sometimes half a mile away. They would skim the water as they swept across, rising twenty or thirty feet as they turned. With a beam wind they would slowly overtake the ship, either overhead or on the windward side. When they got a short distance ahead they would swing away fast downwind, curl round and start another run. They seemed to spend most of the time in the air, but a sufficiently attractive piece of refuse would bring them down on to the water. The snow-white with black trimmings of the mature birds is easily recognized compared to the rather dirty grey and brown of the younger ones. Mature birds were seen much less frequently.

Although there was no opportunity to look out for or photograph birds at Tristan da Cunha, the island was a most interesting place. Its hey-day was at the time of the great Indiamen of the East India Company. Like St Helena, Tristan provided fresh water, vegetables and meat in exchange for rope and canvas and all kinds of manufactured things. I went ashore in one of their boats which had a wooden framework covered with canvas. The canvas is painted with penguin-oil to make it waterproof. This saves the precious timber, and makes them very light so that they are easily hauled up the steep beach. One member of our party, not finding anything convenient to sit on in the boat, was about to sit on his shooting-stick when shouts of anguish pointed out the unwisdom of putting the end of a shooting-stick into a canvas hull.

About two hundred and fifty people lived on the island, descended in the most part from one family, which remained on the island after the garrison was withdrawn in 1817, and who were later joined by two ex-Navy men and three stonemasons. Not unnaturally, wives were a bit of a problem, so the men appealed to the Governor of St Helena, who managed to persuade some girls from that island to try their luck on Tristan.

The settlement on the northern shore is called Edinburgh after Prince Alfred, Duke of Edinburgh, Queen Victoria's second son, who visited Tristan in 1867. In the course of his career in the Navy he visited a great many parts of the world, and was the first member of the Royal Family to visit Australia, in 1867, and New Zealand in 1870. In the course of my own journeys I frequently crossed his tracks in the most unlikely places.

The geography of Tristan is simple. Forty-five square miles compared to the two hundred and twenty-five square miles of the Isle of Man, roughly circular with a volcanic crater in the middle and ridges radiating down to cliffs and coves with a sloping plateau on the southern side where the settlement stood. The scenery and the houses were not unlike the west of Scotland. The names of places had an interesting ring about them—there was 'The Place Where the Minister Landed His Things', 'Nellie's Hump' and 'The Point-Where-the-Goat-Jumped-Off'.

There were sheep, communally owned, a few cattle and a great many geese and donkeys, but potatoes formed the staple diet.

There were virtually no wild animals except some cats; Fur Seals and sea-elephants are found along the shores and penguins on a very small rocky island, about half a mile from Tristan. There are plenty of fish in the waters and in recent times a small crawfish cannery was established. This had caused a major economic upheaval because some of the islanders, employed by the cannery, now earned money, and this was something quite new to the island which had never needed any before.

In order to keep the world informed of our activities we used to send off news bulletins every now and then. I think the bulletin for our day at Tristan is worth reproducing:

> Tristan da Cunha was a most impressive sight when we anchored at 0930 this morning. For a brief moment the 7,000-foot peak above the sheer cliffs appeared through a break in the almost permanent cloud that surmounts this very inaccessible island.
>
> It was bright with a fresh breeze and immediately the long boats of the fishermen put off and sailed out to us, bringing with them the Administrator, Mr Forsyth-Thompson, and his wife, and the Chief of the island, Mr Willie Repetto.
>
> The Duke of Edinburgh, dressed as an Admiral of the Fleet and accompanied

by the Chief, boarded one of the long boats and at the Chief's invitation took the helm and sailed the long boat ashore. On the beach he was greeted with the cheers of the fishermen while the womenfolk of the island added theirs from the cliff top.

Behind the beach stood the canning factory for the island's main industry—crawfish—which His Royal Highness inspected on the way to the settlement. An amusing spectacle was the transporting of the instruments of the Royal Marine band by ox-wagons from the beach. After climbing a cliff-side track Prince Philip arrived at a beautifully decorated archway of welcome, where he was greeted by Dr and Mrs Gooch, Mr Stapleford, the agricultural adviser, and his wife, and Mr Harding, the schoolmaster, and his wife. Donkeys, usually a familiar feature of the island, were absent, having been driven to the other side of the island lest they should eat the arch of welcome.

His Royal Highness was conducted by the Chief and the Administrator to a succession of croft-like thatched cottages where he saw groups of the women colourfully dressed in their best clothes carding and spinning wool. It was in one of these cottages that Prince Philip received a special welcome from Martha Repetto, the head-woman of Tristan. Next door he was shown an exhibition of the crafts of the island. This included amongst samples of island knitted clothing, models of boats and marbles made from eyes of dried bluefish. There should have been six of these, but the Chief's cat had swallowed two of them the night before.

Before going to the Library for a reception of the islanders, Prince Philip visited the church, where he was shown an ensign given by H.M.S. *Magpie* during her last visit a year ago. After lunch at the Administrator's house, Prince Philip saw the school, and then walked to the site of the new hall. The whole community was assembled there for the laying of the commemorative stone. Fallen in in front of the dais was a guard of honour of Brownies, Girl Guides and Sea Scouts, and after the Administrator and the Chief had delivered speeches of loyalty to the Queen and of welcome, His Royal Highness laid the stone and presented to the islanders a battery-powered record player with amplifiers. His Royal Highness accepted from the Chief several beautiful and representative presents from the island. He left to see the Store, a miniature agricultural show, the hospital and then a football match between the island and the ship's company of *Britannia*. The game was played on what can only be called a rugged pitch which gave a distinct advantage to the side playing downhill, so long as they were able to pull up before the cliff edge. The islanders, dressed in long white trousers tucked into football socks, looked like a team of Morris dancers, and displayed an agile knowledge of the tricky terrain. The enthusiastic crowd gave vent to such cries of 'Keep it on the island' and 'Mind the precipice'. The game, which gave great amusement to all, ended most satisfactorily at 2–2.

In the School Hall Prince Philip and his party joined in the island dancing, and the music was provided by the Royal Marine band and the local accordion band alternately. This ended a particularly colourful and unusual day and His Royal Highness was given an enthusiastic farewell before entering the long boat for *Britannia*.

In October 1961, after everyone had thought that the volcano had been extinct for centuries, Tristan da Cunha started to erupt. The community escaped to Nightingale Island leaving all their possessions behind. After thirty-six very uncomfortable hours on the rocky islet they were rescued by a Dutch liner, the *Tjisadane*. Eventually the Islanders arrived in England to start a new life.

I was particularly interested to see Gough Island because, only a few years before, I had given some help to a scientific expedition to spend a few months on the island. They made the first comprehensive survey of this little volcanic peak and Martin Holdgate, a member of the expedition, very kindly sent me a copy of his book about the island, *Mountains in the Sea.* Consequently the place already seemed familiar when we got there. The book described the frequent occasions when it was impossible to land on their boulder beach, so we were not very confident about our chances, particularly as we could only afford to stay about twenty-four hours. As luck would have it, conditions were ideal and we all got ashore without getting too wet and without damaging the dinghy.

The island was originally called Diego Alvarez by the Portuguese in the sixteenth century. Later, in 1731, it was rediscovered by a certain Captain Gough. It has never been inhabited, but there are many inscriptions on the rock-faces to record visits by whalemen, sealers and optimistic diamond miners.

Eight miles long by four miles wide, rising to Edinburgh (not Prince Alfred this time) Peak, just under 3,000 feet, the whole island is green and there are streams tumbling through the overgrown valleys and tussock-grass or dropping over sheer cliffs into the sea.

Gough has an enormous population of nesting seabirds, but it has also a flourishing Rock-hopper Penguin rookery, a colony of flightless rails, peculiar to the island, and a vast number of mice.

It was as we steamed towards Gough that we saw the great raft of sea-birds, mostly Sooty Shearwaters, covering several acres on the gentle swell. According to W. B. Alexander in his *Birds of the Ocean*—essential for bird-watchers anywhere at sea—'Both sexes (petrels, shearwaters and fulmars) take part in incubation, one remaining silently in the burrow all day whilst its mate ranges the ocean for food. Just at dusk the foraging birds begin to return. . . .' I can only imagine that the 'foraging birds' had collected enough food and were gathered waiting for dusk and the change-over. The change-over is done in the dark, presumably to avoid the attentions of the Great Skuas.

Most of the burrowing birds have such weak legs that they have to shuffle along the ground on their breasts with the help of their wings, when they must be highly vulnerable to skuas.

All the seabirds which nest on the island spend most of their lives far out of sight of land, and it is still a mystery how they manage to find this speck of land in the southern mid-Atlantic ridge and return to it every year. Some of the petrels in particular are known to migrate right across the Equator to the northern hemisphere. Although the migratory routes have not been thoroughly investigated, they appear to be just as definite as those of land birds.

Gough is obviously very popular with seabirds as a desirable nesting-place, and Martin Holdgate gives on p. 30 a list of the birds which either nest on or visit the island.

The Tristan names are probably those used by seamen long ago or corruptions of them. Of this list we only recognized the shearwaters, skuas, Sooty Albatrosses, the flightless rail, the bunting and the Rock-hoppers. These penguins are most delightful birds; all penguins are fascinating to me, but these little Rock-hoppers are the most enjoyable and amusing to watch. The incongruous long yellow feathers on either side of their heads give them the look of small and very serious costermongers. The constant coming and going up and down the little stream between the sea and the rookery is a splendid sight as they hop and splash and wriggle in single file. They really do hop, keeping both feet together.

The only people on the island were four South African meteorologists who had taken over the survey party's hut. Their six Dorper sheep and Australorp fowls made strange-looking companions for the penguins.

Our visit to the island turned out to be very timely as one of the South Africans was found to be suffering from an infected appendix. The Yacht's sick-bay staff whipped it out in no time.

Before leaving we sighted some Fur Seals and two southern Right Whales who seemed to be having a high old time in the bay. I tried to get a photograph of them as they leapt clean out of the water. Unfortunately I only had one exposure left, and then when I changed films the show was over. The one exposure did in fact show a whale right out of the water, but the negative got damaged by mistake in the dark room.

Although the Falkland Islands lie on about the same latitude as South

A List of Birds of Gough Island

USUAL NAME	LATIN NAME	TRISTAN NAME	STATUS
Rock-hopper Penguin	*Eudyptes crestatus*	Pinnamin	Extremely abundant
Tristan Wandering Albatross	*Diomedea exulans dabbenena*	Gony	Common
Yellow-nosed Albatross	*Diomedea chlororhynchos*	Molly	Abundant
Sooty Albatross	*Phoebetria fusca*	Peeoo	Abundant
Light-mantled Sooty Albatross	*Phoebetria palpebrata*		Rare visitor
Black-browed Albatross	*Diomedea melanophris*		Rare visitor
Giant Petrel	*Macronectes giganteus*	Nelly, Stinker	Common
Broad-billed Prion	*Pachyptila vittata*	Nightbird	Extremely abundant
White-chinned Petrel	*Procellaria aequinoctialis*	Ring-eye, Cape Hen	Uncommon
Great Grey Petrel	*Adamaster cinereus*	Pediunker	Abundant
Greater Shearwater	*Puffinus gravis*	Petrel	Abundant
Dusky Shearwater	*Puffinus assimilis*	Whistler	Extremely abundant
Great-winged Petrel	*Pterodroma macroptera*	Black Haglet	Abundant
Atlantic Petrel	*Pterodroma incerta*	White-breasted Black Haglet	Abundant
Kerguelen Petrel	*Pterodroma brevirostris*	Blue Nighthawk	Extremely abundant
Soft-plumaged Petrel	*Pterodroma mollis*	Nighthawk	Extremely abundant
Cape Pigeon	*Daption capensis*		Rare visitor
Wilson's Petrel	*Oceanites oceanicus*	Skipjack	Rare visitor
White-faced Storm Petrel	*Pelagodroma marina*	Skipjack	Common
White-bellied Storm Petrel	*Fregetta grallaria*	Skipjack	Abundant
Grey-backed Storm Petrel	*Garrodia nereis*	Skipjack	Abundant
Tristan Diving Petrel	*Pelecanoides urinatrix dacunhae*	Flying Pinnamin	Abundant
Tristan Skua	*Catharacta skua hamiltoni*	Seahen	Abundant
Kelp Gull	*Larus dominicanus*		Rare visitor
Swallow-tailed Tern	*Sterna vittata*	King-Bird	Abundant
Common Noddy	*Anous stolidus*	Wood pigeon	Common
Gough Island Moorhen	*Porphyriornis comeri*	Island Cock	Common
Gough Island Bunting	*Rowettia goughensis*	Starchy	Abundant

Georgia their climate is more temperate and you only find a few of the proper Antarctic birds and animals there. The two main islands are known as East and West Falkland and they are about the same size. The capital, Port Stanley, is on the East Island. The country and the light and also the general atmosphere is very like that of the Outer Hebrides. There is a bit of general farming, but on the whole everything depends upon sheep.

Taking pictures at sea, or landing from a boat within half a mile of a penguin rookery is photography made easy. An expedition, organized by the Governor, to see a bit of the country and to photograph some birds in the Falkland Islands is quite a different matter.

There are very few roads on the islands so that most of the travelling is done on horseback. The Governor was a particularly keen rider and persuaded me that I could not leave the Falklands without an experience of their variation of this form of transport. As he promised to show me various animals and birds I took my camera with me. The Hasselblad camera in its case with lenses and so on is about the size of an ordinary portable radio and just about as portable. After two hundred yards on my pony I felt very sorry for anyone who has to carry large and awkward camera-cases about; in fact, I thought the whole thing was a great mistake. To begin with, I hadn't been on a horse for nearly six months, and these ponies were as near square as any animal can get, and they were saddled in South American fashion. This consists of two sausage-like pads laced together so that they lie on either side of the horse's backbone. These are then covered with a thick sheepskin which is secured in some mysterious fashion and stirrups appear out of the sheepskin. So long as the pony is stationary this is not an uncomfortable arrangement. In motion, however, one becomes intimately aware of every muscular movement of the pony. Added to this, the ponies apparently neither trot nor canter; I can only describe their progress as running. The country we crossed was ordinary peaty moorland with the usual clumps of heather and boggy holes so that it seemed as if the pony's legs were entirely uncoordinated with each other. They certainly covered the ground at a respectable speed, but I found it more than difficult to accommodate myself to the motion, particularly as by then I had the camera-case strap around my neck with the case dancing about in my lap. Under normal circumstances and with a bit of practice, it might have been reasonably tolerable, but at that moment I fondly wished that God had never invented a horse.

In every other respect the expedition was a great success. It was a lovely clear sunny day with a sparkling vivid blue sea against black rocks, dark brown seaweed and almost white sandy beaches, with a background of gently rolling grass and heather-covered hills. There were cormorants and Magellan Penguins, Logger or Steamer Duck and dolphins. Luckily they all proved to be patient sitters, and I got several good pictures. I discovered, incidentally, that trying to take photographs of dolphins jumping out of the water is one of the most extravagant forms of photo-graphy unless you want to make a collection of square pictures of disturbed water. It is virtually impossible to have everything ready and pointing at the right place at the right time, although I went on thinking I could for much too long.

The Magellan Penguins and the Logger Duck were on one of the little beaches, but there was no cover near enough to make stalking worth while, so it had to be 'grandmother's footsteps' again. This time, consider-ing what I must have looked like on all-fours over an open beach, I think it was most considerate of the birds to stick it as long as they did.

The Logger Duck are flightless birds, even though they look like ordinary duck, and if pursued they can dive for short periods. One evening there was a very nice breeze blowing in Stanley Bay, so we took out the little 'Flying Fifteen' sailing boat *Coweslip* and went for a sail. We came across a party of these duck, minding their own business, but we decided to see what happened if we chased them. We went faster than they did, but they were much more manœuvrable and when things looked really serious they dived. We kept this up for some time, wondering when it would dawn on them that we could not go straight into the wind, but apparently they were more intelligent than that; they swam for some rocks.

In the days of the windjammers, the Falkland Islands must have seemed to many a seaman, lashed and battered by the gales of Cape Horn, as a miraculous haven of peace. To many others the islands proved to be the graveyard of their ships. Dismasted and leaking, they were beached in the comparative quiet of the inlets and the remains of these great ships are still to be seen in almost every bay and creek. There is still a hulk of one of them afloat in Port Stanley, but I don't know her name or her story.

The Black-browed Albatross, shown in the arms of Commander Adams (plate 23), was found squatting on deck one morning near the Falkland Islands. All these large seabirds need a slope or a cliff to allow them to take off, because their legs are too weak to spring them into the air and their wings are too long to flap when they are on the ground. Although the deck was quite large, the guard-rails effectively prevented the bird from getting away.

The bird was reasonably docile when picked up, but we took no chances with that powerful six-inch beak with its cruel hook and the two five-foot wings. It is only when these large birds are seen against something familiar that their very considerable size becomes obvious; flying, they look no bigger than average gulls.

Launching it was no great problem; we simply took it on to the wing of the bridge and threw it over the side. It dropped no more than a couple of feet before spreading its wings and sailing off to sea as if nothing had happened.

The names of these seabirds are rather confusing because sailors are not well known for being able to tell the difference between the many kinds of birds, so that similar names were used for different birds by seamen of different nations. According to Alexander, for instance, 'Sailors not infrequently call these brown birds [immature albatross] Mollymawks, Mollyhawks, or Mollymokes, names which they also sometimes apply to other large brownish seabirds such as the Giant Petrel, Skuas or immature gulls. What are more usually called Mollymawks are the smaller species of albatross.' Rightly or wrongly we called the Black-browed Albatross a Mollymawk. Alexander goes on to say: 'Gony or Goony is another name frequently applied to birds of this family by seamen.' He also has some interesting things to say about the derivation of some of the names: 'The name Albatross is a corruption of the Spanish (originally Moorish) word *Alcatraz* (i.e. Pelican), and has nothing to do with the whiteness of the bird as is sometimes supposed. Mollymawk is a corruption of the Dutch *Mallemuck*, derived from "mal" (foolish) and "mok" (gull); whilst Gony is an English dialect word for a simpleton or booby.'

Shearwaters get their name from their habit of skimming low over the waves, and some believe that the term petrel may be an allusion to St Peter's attempt to walk on the water. Seamen generally only apply the name petrel to the Storm Petrels, or 'Mother Carey's Chickens', a corruption of 'Mater Cara'—a name for the Virgin Mary. The presence of these birds near a ship is taken to herald a storm, which seems rather contradictory. The Giant Petrel is known as a Nelly or sometimes as a Stinker —we preferred the latter name. Other petrels are known as Cape Hens

(White-chinned), Cape Pigeons (Pintado) and Cape Dove (Brown Petrel). Fulmar derives from 'fowl mew' or gull, owing to its characteristic musky scent which remains very strong on its breeding grounds.

The prions are generally known as Ice-birds or Whale-birds, while shear-waters are sometimes known as Mutton Birds or Hags. In New Zealand waters the Sooty Shearwater is known as a Mutton Bird, which derives from the Maori custom, in the southern parts of South Island, of taking the fat young birds from their nests for food. The people of St Kilda also used to indulge in this, and I believe it is still done occasionally in Iceland.

Again, according to Alexander, 'The name "Penguin" was originally applied to the Great Auk or Garefowl of the North Atlantic. On the discovery of similar flightless birds in the southern Hemisphere the name was very naturally applied to them also, and, with the extinction of the northern bird, has now become theirs alone!'

Seamen are not natural ornithologists.

SECTION THREE

Sub-Antarctic and Antarctic

ALL the stories of the wild seas, cold stormy climate and barren lands, would lead one to believe that no living thing would willingly go anywhere near this area. Yet here I saw a greater variety of birds and in greater numbers than anywhere else.

In the sea, just where the really cold Antarctic water meets the warmer Atlantic, the big whales live and breed. There are two main kinds of whale: the Sperm Whale with its huge head and long lower jaw amply supplied with very business-like teeth; and the Baleen Whales which have enormous mouths filled with what seems to be a kind of bony broom, used at one time for stiffening ladies' stays. This fringe enables them to trap their food inside as they push the water out through the broom which acts as a sieve. The biggest Baleen Whales—the Blue Whale—can be anything up to ninety or one hundred feet long. The Sperm Whales are usually smaller.

The Baleen Whales feed on the Euphasia Shrimp which congregates in huge numbers where the cold waters of the Antarctic seas meet the relatively warmer water of the South Atlantic. These small pinkish creatures are particularly fond of icebergs, and when these capsize, because of uneven melting, the parts which come up from under the water look quite pink with the number of shrimps still clinging to them.

Sperm Whales feed on the giant squid which live at great depths in much the same areas. Titanic battles have been described between these monsters of the ocean, and many of the Sperm Whales caught have shown scars of these encounters. The Sperm Whale is one of the few inhabitants of the seas prepared to take on the great sharks and Killer Whales.

Baleen Whales sink when they are killed, but Sperm Whales float. This meant that the old sailing-ship whalers could only take Sperm Whales, which they could cut up alongside the ship or haul up on to a beach. Almost every beach I saw in the Antarctic was littered with the gigantic whitened bones of the whales whose carcasses had been washed or dragged ashore in years gone by.

Modern whalers still take Sperm Whales when they can get them, but their main catch is Blue and Fin Whales, which they have to pump up with compressed air in order to keep them afloat. They are then towed to the factory ship or whale factory ashore, where they are hauled up a slipway on to the flensing deck to be expertly cut up for boiling. About 90 per cent of every whale is usefully employed either as oil, which is the main reason for catching them, or as bone and blood meal.

I visited the whale factory ship *Southern Harvester* just inside the Antarctic Circle at the eastern end of the Bellingshausen Sea, nearly 800 miles south of Cape Horn. The weather, strangely enough, would not have disgraced the Mediterranean.

The method of transfer was quite interesting. A whale-catcher, towing a dead Sperm Whale alongside as a fender, came alongside the Yacht. On the catcher's deck was a large round wicker basket which was attached to a rope which went to the top of the catcher's mast and then down to its winch. There were also two steadying lines. The basket was hauled up and then across to the Yacht; each member of the party in turn climbed in the basket, was hauled up off the Yacht's deck and lowered on to the catcher.

This sounds quite reasonable, but there was quite a swell running and the catcher's mast reached only a short way above the Yacht's deck. The result was that as the ships rolled apart the basket was snatched away from the Yacht, and then swung gaily about the catcher's mast. The return journey was done the same way and was even more perilous. Added to this, each time the ships rolled together the Sperm Whale fender was given a hefty squeeze and as it was not altogether freshly killed the waves of stench that arose at intervals cannot be described.

The factory ship acts as a depot for about fifteen to twenty whale-catchers which are not unlike the ordinary East Coast trawler. High bows and a very low freeboard, a single tall funnel, and big steam engines to give them at least fifteen knots. The harpoon gun is right in the eyes of the ship, and the line runs from the harpoon to the top of the mast and then down into the forward hold over an arrangement of springs and pulleys, which acts in the same way as the bend in a fishing-rod, before reaching the winch, which acts like the fisherman's reel. The gunner commands the catcher and is almost invariably Norwegian.

Blue Whales are no great problem to catch because they dive and surface to blow more or less in a straight line. The Fin Whale, on the other hand, dives in one direction and usually surfaces in quite another. On one occasion *Britannia* followed a whale-catcher as she tried to harpoon a Fin Whale. The chase went on for two hours and the whale had not been caught by the time we had to leave.

The harpoon has an explosive head and in addition four prongs come out to prevent the harpoon being withdrawn. In most cases the whale is killed almost at once, and it is only a matter of reeling it in. As soon as it is within reach, a compressed-air hose is inserted into the whale and it is blown up to prevent it from sinking. Markers are attached for visual and radar recovery and the whale is cast adrift. When a catcher has accumulated a sufficient number of whales it collects them and tows them back to the factory ship. These ships, which displace about 10,000 tons, have an enormous square hole at the waterline in their sterns and a ramp which leads from the hole up to the flensing deck, covering about three-quarters of the ship's space. The deck is divided into two parts. On the first part the flensers get to work with long curved knives on the ends of broom-handles and cut the blubber off the flesh. It is cut in strips and the strips are torn off by a wire and a steam winch while the flenser neatly separates the blubber from the flesh as the strip peels off. The long strips are then cut into roughly one-foot squares and pushed into the tops of the boiling vats. These holes are level with the deck, so it is advisable to look where you are going on the flensing deck, particularly as the blood and blubber make it as slippery as an ice-rink.

The remainder of the whale, that is, the flesh and bones after the blubber has been stripped, is dragged by winches on to the second part of the deck, where it is, so to speak, butchered. The flesh is sliced off in huge hunks, cut up and pushed into one set of boiling vats, and the bones into another.

All the parts of the whale are perfectly recognizable, but their size comes as a bit of a shock. The vertebrae, for instance, are the size of side-drums and are wrenched apart by steam winches. The ribs go up to ten feet; as an ordinary butcher's saw wouldn't get very far on those bones, they use a steam-driven saw with a blade eight feet long. The intestines look very like a heap of inner-tubes for tractors' tyres.

Apart from accommodation, the rest of the ship is given over to the machinery for processing the whales to oil, and bone and blood meal and the necessary storage tanks and holds.

The whaling stations ashore are equipped in the same way, but instead of being squeezed into a limited space the different departments are spread out conveniently. Ashore or afloat, whale factories have a smell all of their own which has to be experienced to be properly appreciated.

The whale-catchers and the factory ship have a constant attendance of large numbers of seabirds of all sorts: albatrosses, Giant Petrels, or Stinkers, the smaller petrels and prions, gulls and terns. The attraction is the odd bits of blubber and waste which get washed overboard and the carcasses themselves as they float in huge bunches on either side of the factory ship waiting to be dealt with.

Between South Georgia and the South Shetlands we sometimes had quite large flocks of Pintado Petrels or Cape Pigeons, or perhaps several Giant Petrels, and then nothing for a day or two till we picked up a party of albatrosses. I always enjoyed the Sooty Albatross which is a sort of milk-chocolate colour, rather smaller than the Wanderer but it has a much kinder expression. Unfortunately, they are rather shy, and none came very close and if they are photographed against the sea they become virtually invisible. If taken against the sky they just look black.

By far the most difficult birds to capture on film are the little prions or whalebirds. They seem to fly at great speed without any particular pattern, and as they are so small they are only noticed when they get reasonably close, by which time it is usually too late to get them. We were in these high latitudes in the early days of January (midsummer in the Antarctic), but even so the weather was never exactly warm so that after an hour or two vainly trying to catch up with these little birds my fingers became so numb that I would press the shutter button quite unintentionally, simply because I couldn't feel it.

It is difficult to believe that South Georgia, with its snow-covered mountains, treeless landscape and huge icebergs floating in its bays, is the same distance south of the Equator as Manchester is north of it. The Gulf Stream doesn't always get the appreciation which it deserves.

South Georgia is a really spectacular island with peaks reaching nearly 10,000 feet, twinkling in the sun but gloomy and threatening under stormy clouds. The mountains plunge straight into the sea on the south side of the island, but on the north side there are some wonderful natural harbours and quite a lot of low-lying ground. It is in one of these harbours that the whale factory at Grytviken is established and operates during the summer months. Shackleton died at this station and it was also the end of his fantastic journey from Elephant Island in 1915.

His ship, the *Endurance*, got jammed in the ice of the Weddell Sea and was finally crushed. He rescued the boats and dragged them across the ice and eventually reached Elephant Island just off the northern tip of the Graham Land Peninsula. The season was getting on and the party was unlikely to survive the winter and even if they did they would still be 600 miles from the nearest habitation. Shackleton decided to set off with a small party and get help as soon as possible.

Although the Falkland Islands were nearest, they lay due north across the Drake Straits through which the wind and seas are funnelled from the Pacific to the Atlantic. He had no hope of sailing across those straits in a small open boat. On the other hand, South Georgia was about twice as far away but it lay almost directly to leeward and so offered him a very much better chance. They cannibalized two of their three boats, and using their sails and woodwork to deck-in the *James Caird* and make it reasonably seaworthy, there was a faint possibility that it might reach South Georgia. Shackleton set off with five men and navigated that frail cockleshell, twenty-two feet six inches long and with a six-foot beam, through virtually ceaseless gales to an island barely a hundred miles long and about a thousand miles away. It took them sixteen terrible days and nights, and then they just managed to scramble ashore on the steep south side of the island. The whaling station lay on the north side with unmapped snow- and ice-covered mountains in between. It sounds almost incredible, but they simply walked across in thirty-six hours, and when they arrived at the station manager's office no one would believe their story. Quite apart from the distance involved at the end of a gruelling sea journey, the crossing of South Georgia was a first-class feat of alpine mountaineering in itself. I stood by his memorial, looking at those mountains and I've some idea of the sort of seamanship and navigation the boat journey entailed—I wouldn't have believed his story either. Soon afterwards he was able to get to the Falkland Islands and arrange for the rescue of the rest of the party on Elephant Island. Before the expedition, Queen Alexandra had given him a Union Jack, which he carried with him throughout the journey and the return to England. It hangs in Sandringham to this day.

There is another Antarctic memento in the Yacht. Scott's companion on his last expedition, the late Lord Mountevans, gave King George V the little silk white ensign which always flew from Scott's personal sledge. The King kept the tattered little flag framed in his cabin in the *Victoria and Albert*, and when she was broken up it was transferred to *Britannia*.

Shackleton went back to South Georgia on another expedition in 1922 and died there. He is buried in a little cemetery just outside the whaling station, and there is a memorial to him on the headland at the entrance to the bay. His name is still a legend with the men who go whaling.

South Georgia is a wonderful place for seabirds of all kinds, and Ian Rankin in his book *Antarctic Island* gives a very complete account of the bird life at different times of the year. We didn't have much time to spare, but I did manage an expedition to a King Penguin rookery where we also found Adélie, Gentoo and Chinstrap Penguins. The name Chinstrap may sound odd, but it is most descriptive as they have black heads and white chins with a thin black line running under them.

We also found quite a number of Elephant Seals on the beach. Huge, slug-like creatures, ten to twelve feet long, with none of the charm of the Fur Seals. They weren't particularly disturbed by us, but if we got too close the males somehow expanded and extended their noses (hence their name, no doubt), opened their mouths wide and made a noise like a particularly fruity belch. The young are more attractive, and we found one about four foot long, pale grey, fast asleep in a comfortable hollow of an old bleached whalebone.

The King Penguins are splendid birds, with their brightly coloured heads and shiny dark grey and white coats. They all seem so neatly turned out, except for rather tattered imitation fur-coats worn by the young, which reach from their necks to their ankles.

Penguins are not very fast on land and as they are not particularly afraid, it is possible to get right up to them and even hold their flippers. They don't like this much and they let you hold them with good-mannered reluctance. Adélie Penguins are rather rough and rude creatures, while the Kings are infinitely the most dignified.

There is a theory that because both sexes appear to be identical, penguins must have matrimonial problems of a very special kind and that mating occurs somehow by trial and error. I find this difficult and rather depressing to believe. However, there is no doubt that courtship consists of offering small flat stones to each other for the purpose of making what passes for a nest. Cases have been reported of penguins offering stones to visiting humans. This didn't happen to me, but if penguins cannot tell the difference between humans and themselves there may be some basis of truth in the theory of trial and error. Whichever way they use for solving their problems, the eggs appear, are incubated by the parents in turn, and are hatched. The King and Emperor Penguins lay one egg which is hatched on their feet under a fold of skin which forms a pouch over it. When it is time to transfer the egg to the other parent a very tricky manœuvre is involved. Strangely enough the Emperor Penguin, according to W. B. Alexander, 'chooses the perpetual darkness of the Antarctic winter as the period and the ice-barrier as the scene of the operation'.

Apsley Cherry-Garrard, who took part in Scott's last Antarctic expedition in 1909, describes in *The Worst Journey in the World* how three men set out in the mid-winter darkness in temperatures that dropped to $-70°$F and in constant gales of wind and snow to find the Emperor Penguin colony on Cape Crozier and to bring back some of their eggs. They brought back three after dreadful difficulties and when he eventually delivered them to the British Museum, the Keeper of the Egg Collection just told him to put them on the table and when the 'Heroic Explorer' (Cherry-Garrard's description) didn't leave at once, the Keeper dismissed him with 'You needn't wait.'

It seems incredible that it should be necessary for these birds to incubate and hatch their young in the middle of the Antarctic winter. The reason is that they are large birds and grow slowly so that unless the young are born early in the year they are not sufficiently strong to survive the next winter on their own.

Penguins may be clumsy on land, but in the sea they are almost as fast as seals and porpoises. If they are really in a hurry they leap out of the water and dive in again some four or five feet farther on. We saw this happening close to the Yacht in Admiralty Bay in the South Shetlands. They can leap three or four feet up on to rock-ledges or ice-floes, which makes them look as if they had been jerked out on strings.

The rookery may contain any number of birds, and the ones I saw must have had two or three thousand birds sitting and squabbling or making their way on their feet or on their tummies to and from the sea. Where there is snow they simply flop forward and toboggan down the slope. Progress upwards is much more laborious. When they get to the water's edge they always seem reluctant to get in—like bathers when the water is too cold. Eventually one of a group gets jostled in, and all the others peer over to see what happens. This caution is dictated by the possible presence and appetite of the Leopard Seal, which is said to catch and skin penguins in one movement and toss the skin back into the air.

The South Shetland Islands lie just off the Graham Land Peninsula and continue on beyond it to the north-east. There is an idea that the Falkland Islands, South Georgia, the South Sandwich, the South Orkneys, the South Shetlands and Graham Land are all part of the Andes chain which has been bent into an arc eastwards towards the South Atlantic, and gaps forced into it by the pounding seas of the South Pacific.

I didn't see a very great deal of the South Shetlands, but they certainly didn't get their name from any similarity to the northern Shetlands. As mountainous as South Georgia but without even the leaven of the sparse vegetation and moorland of that island, they lie stark and forbidding in the most dangerous seas of the world. At one time in prehistory they must have been green and fertile, because at the Survey Base at Admiralty Bay they showed us fossils of fern-like leaves which they had found in the vicinity. We found this quite easy to believe as we passed them in relatively fine weather. As they are now, the black and white of towering rock and ice made a magnificent backdrop to the Pintado Petrels which kept us company in that area.

On our way to the Survey Base in Admiralty Bay we managed a short expedition to an enormous Gentoo Penguin rookery. As usual we found a party of Elephant Seals taking it easy on the beach. Much later, back in London, I gave a talk about this journey to a lot of school children in the Festival Hall. One reporter noted that I had referred to the overpowering smell of the whale factory and also to the very considerable pong of large penguin rookeries and Elephant Seal dormitories, and concluded that I must have a very sensitive nose. At the risk of encouraging the myth I must in all fairness report that penguin rookeries and Elephant Seal dormitories do have a most unpleasant odour, and I strongly recommend anyone interested to approach them from upwind.

The most remarkable island in this group is Deception Island. I imagine it got its name because it is roughly circular with cliffs or steep slopes dropping into the sea apparently all around it. In fact, it is an old volcanic crater, but at one point on its perimeter the side has collapsed and there is a steep narrow entrance, called Neptune's Bellows, leading into a wonderfully protected anchorage inside. We arrived off the entrance in a thick fog, and in order to get ashore I got into one of the Yacht's motor-boats which was then guided through the gap by radio-telephone, using the Yacht's radar. The entrance is steep and narrow and we were not particularly encouraged by the sight of a whale-catcher stuck fast on the rocks at the narrowest point.

The picture inside is one of utter desolation. There is virtually no vegetation, the rocky slopes are barren with odd patches of snow and ice which merely make the place look even more untidy. Apart from the base huts the only signs of human habitation don't improve the look of it either. There is a derelict whale factory and a partly eroded cemetery. Hauled up incongruously on the beach were two Catalina flying-boats which belonged to an aerial survey party based at Deception. The beach is of fine black sand and the last vestiges of volcanic activity keep it warm, so that in the cold air thin wisps of steam drift about between the huge bleached skeletons of long-dead whales.

It was here that the Yacht was visited by three Sheathbills which hopped about on the guard-rails with great confidence. They are quite unlike any other seabird as they are pure white and look more like bantams than anything else.

That evening I invited all the Survey and Base parties for drinks and a film. I showed them *Seven Brides for Seven Brothers*, but I'm not sure whether it was a good idea or whether it was perhaps slightly misjudged.

Unlike the Arctic which is all sea, the Antarctic is a continent. Roughly circular in shape, it is pinched in by the Ross Sea south of New Zealand, and the Weddell Sea to the south of South Georgia. Directly opposite Cape Horn the Graham Land Peninsula sticks out like a bent finger into the Drake Straits.

The continent is claimed by slices from the South Pole. From 20° west to 80° west it is claimed by Britain, from 80° west to 150° west it is claimed by the United States, from 20° west to 45° east it is claimed by Norway; the rest, apart from a small French slice of Adélie Land, is divided between New Zealand and Australia.

Slices of influence are arranged differently in the Arctic. The slices are decided by the width of the countries nearest the Pole. Canada, for instance, would claim a slice between the longitude of the border with Alaska to the farthest point which her territory overlaps Greenland. If this system were used for the Antarctic, there would be an entirely different situation and in fact the countries of South America base their claims to the Antarctic upon the Arctic system. This produces almost endless arguments.

Even the name Graham Land Peninsula is not universally accepted.

The Americans call it the Palmer Peninsula after the American whaling and sealing captain who discovered it. The British called it after the current First Lord of the Admiralty some years later.

The British slice of the Antarctic is administered by the Falkland Islands, and at the moment the only activity in the area is by a number of Survey parties which spend a year at a time at various bases on the Graham Land Peninsula and the South Shetland Islands; their duties are mapping, charting, geological surveying and weather reporting, and all the bases which I visited seemed to find the work and the life hard but interesting and rewarding.

My visit coincided with the annual change-over of base parties. The *John Biscoe* was specially designed for this work. Strengthened against ice, she is also fitted to carry the stores for the bases and the accommodation for those going out and those returning from their year's spell of duty. This change-over can only take place in summer when the weather is reasonably fine and the sea-ice is melted.

I spent a few days in the *John Biscoe*, and in her I visited one of the two bases inside the Antarctic circle. For some curious reason one of the passengers had brought a couple of tennis rackets, and some balls, and so with great solemnity and not a little hilarity the only recorded game of tennis in the Antarctic was played outside the base hut. I seem to remember that the Antarctic Tennis Club was formed, but as far as I know, it has never been recognized by the Lawn Tennis Association.

Quite close to this base there was an Adélie Penguin rookery, and we spent a very pleasant half-hour paying it a visit. The Adélies are the toughs of the penguin world, but even so they have a lot of charm. They will resist any interference with their incubation or their chicks, with raised hackles and much pecking, but they are soon pacified and quite prepared to treat visiting humans as equals.

It would be hard to imagine a bleaker situation for a nesting site. Mostly snow, with haphazard patches of rock and gravel sticking out, they are usually about fifty feet or so above the water. For some reason the sea looks pitch-black and it is pock-marked with slabs of grey sea-ice and blue-green 'chips' of the ice-barrier icebergs.

The sea-ice is relatively soft because it just forms on the sea: the icebergs are very hard indeed because the ice has been formed under the immense pressure of thousands of feet of snow before it breaks off into the sea. The *John Biscoe* sloshed through sea-ice four feet thick without a judder, but every time she hit a bit of hard ice she made a clang like a blacksmith's anvil. The flat slabs of sea-ice frequently had Weddell Seals resting on them.

At one of these bases I was given a ride in a dog-drawn sledge. These are used by the surveying parties in winter when the sea is frozen over. Ten feet long, they are drawn by five or six husky dogs and carry the needs of three men. My expedition was all of half a mile.

At another base we walked up a slope to get a better view and were promptly attacked by skuas. This happened at several places, including a penguin rookery. I imagine we must have approached too close to their nests, but I never saw one. In their swoops they never actually struck anybody, but he was a brave man who didn't duck as they came past.

Although we spent only a few days in the area I can quite understand the fascination which the Antarctic has for many people. It may be bleak and stark, but it has a kind of lonely, empty beauty which exercises a very strong attraction. Graham Land, in particular, with its steep mountains, icefalls and the ever-changing colour of the snow, must have some of the most glorious scenery anywhere in the world. Given half a chance I would go back, if only to see the penguins and the seabirds again.

1. *H.M.Y.* Britannia *at Gough Island in the South Atlantic.*

2. *The combination which took most of the pictures. The Swedish Hasselblad camera with a 250 mm. lens.*

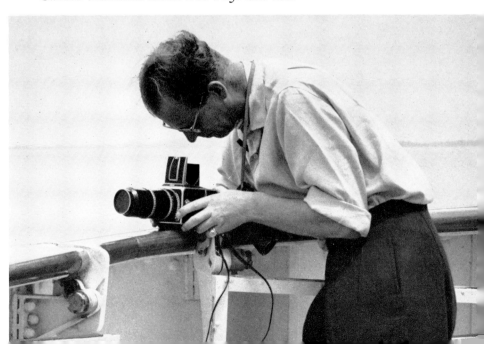

3. Near Ascension Island in the South Atlantic. The Frigate-bird or Man-o'-War Hawk, below, gets its food by forcing other birds to disgorge its meals. It seems to be looking at the Booby above with a speculative eye.

4

4 and 5. Brown Boobies of the South Atlantic are related to the Gannets of the British Isles.

5

6. *Common Noddies, Crested Terns and Sand Crabs. The Crested Terns were a bit shy.*

7. *Common Noddies on the coral beach at Christmas Island in the central Pacific.*

8 and 9. *These show the difference between the Gilbert (upper) and Ellice (lower) outrigger canoes.*

10–12. *The White Tern, a most graceful little bird and a considerate subject.*

13. *Blue-grey Noddies. These two manage to convey a sense of domestic bliss.*

14 and 15. *A female Frigate-bird only let me get so far before unfolding an enormous pair of wings.*

16. *Common Noddies perched in a bush. They seemed to like having their picture taken.*

17. *Occasionally there were other things to do besides taking photographs of birds.*

19. *A White-capped Noddy on its rather untidy nest. Most of the birds on Christmas Island took very little notice of people. This bird cannot have been more than about ten feet away.*

18. *The Wandering Albatross. These almost legendary birds were a constant source of pleasure as they drifted close past the yacht. They accounted for a great deal of exposed film. Incidentally this bird is flying from left to right.*

20–22. *The Adult Wanderer is snow-white with black trimmings. Juveniles come in every shade from a rather tatty brown to a mottled black and grey.*

23. This is a Black-browed Albatross or Molly-mawk; smaller than a Wanderer but this shows the very considerable size of these birds.

24. *Titbits from a whale-catcher attract Wandering Albatrosses, Giant Petrels and Cape Pigeons.*

25. *Rock-hoppers rock hopping against the lush vegetation of Gough Island.*

26. *Rock-hopper Penguins and young at Gough Island. The long head-feathers are bright yellow and orange.*

27. *A great raft of Sooty Shearwaters taking off as they are disturbed by the Yacht. After feeding they gather, waiting for the dark before they can return to burrows on Gough Island safe from marauding Skuas. There is one Great Skua on the right.*

28–31. *Magellan Penguins in the Falkland Islands. Three stages in 'grandmother's footsteps'. They allowed me to get so far and no further before making for the sea. Notice the single Gentoo Penguin in the middle of the top picture, the one with the white spot on the top of its head.*

*32–34. Flightless Logger or Steamer
Duck also feel safer in the water. Beating a
hasty retreat is never very dignified.*

35. *The expedition to photograph the Magellan Penguins and Logger Duck was on horseback. The saddles were something quite novel in my experience.*

36. *Trying to catch a Dolphin out of the water on film is not as easy as it would appear.*

37. *The memorial to Shackleton stands facing the mountains he crossed on his epic journey from Elephant Island.*

38. *The Little Prion or Whale-bird is the smallest of the Petrels, it's not much bigger than a Thrush and a good deal more elusive to photograph.*

39

40

39–41. *Pintado Petrels or Cape Pigeons against the black
and white scenery of the South Shetland Islands.*

41

42. *South Georgia, a fantastic alpine island remote on the edge of the Antarctic. (See over)* ▶

43 and 44. *With underparts mostly white and their black and white backs, Cape Pigeons produce an attractive flickering effect as they swing and roll to and fro across the wake.*

45–50. The Giant Petrel, other-wise known as the Nelly or Stinker, is always in evidence when there is any garbage about or when the whalers drop any titbits of blubber overboard. The habit of trailing their large webbed feet like a badly retracted undercarriage does not make their flight any more graceful.

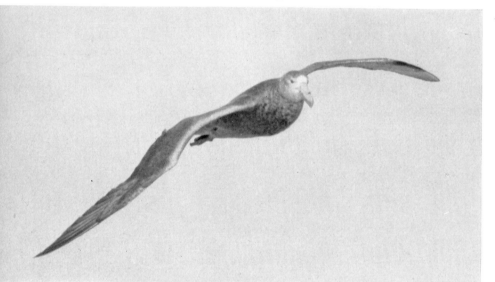

51 and 52. This little party of Sheathbills paid a call on the Yacht at Deception Island.

53. *Elephant Seals are ungainly creatures on land but they can still manage a good scratch.*

54. *This very young Elephant Seal was a little embarrassed at being found asleep in such a remarkable bed.*

55. *Elephant Seal dormitories and Penguin rookeries frequently go together.*

56. *An indignant young Elephant Seal and friend.*

57. *The whale-catcher* Sondra, *typical of the craft which search out and kill the great Blue Whales.*

58. *The* John Biscoe *of the Falkland Islands Dependencies Surveys in the ice of the Antarctic.*

59. Southern Harvester, *whale factory ship and depot for a dozen whale-catchers. The open deck spaces are where the whales are flensed and butchered. The tops of the boiling vats are visible on the left foreground.*

60. *Preparing to transfer by basket from the Yacht to a whale-catcher.*

61. *A dead Sperm Whale acting as a fender between the Yacht and the whale-catcher. The Yacht's side is at the top of the picture and catcher's bulwarks are at the bottom. The chain holds the whale.*

62. *Arriving on board the whale-catcher, twenty feet below the point of departure.*

63. *The Antarctic near the Grahamland peninsula. Dramatic in fine weather,
bleak and dangerous in storms.*

64. *Adelie Penguins do not like interference but they will not leave their nests just because some human comes along.*

65. *The Adelie chicks are covered with a pale grey down.*

66. *Gentoo families. The chicks are almost big enough to fend for themselves but they stick close to Mum—or is it Dad?*

67. 'Don't look now, but there are two dreadful Gentoos trying to horn in.'

69. The young King Penguins look rather uncomfortable in their dressing-gowns.

◄ 68. Part of a King Penguin rookery in South Georgia. Notice the fold of the lower abdomen covering the egg which rests on their web feet.

70 and 71. *King Penguins, beautiful birds with great dignity
and charm.*

72. . . . *and so we say 'farewell' . . .*

About the Birds

A description of the appearance and habits of the
birds shown in the photographs to which the
numbers refer

Booby   Plate 3 *above*
Magnificent Frigate-Bird (*Fregata magnificens*)—Female   *below*

The Magnificent Frigate-Bird ranges from the Galapagos   *Range*
Islands in the Pacific eastwards into the tropical Atlantic.
It is common in the West Indies

The bird in the photograph is a female; its white head   *Note*
indicates that it has not yet achieved full adult plumage.
Females of this species can be distinguished from the female
Great Frigate-Bird as they have the throat black.
The 'Man-o'-war Hawk' is looking upwards at the booby
doubtless with thoughts of an easily gained meal in view.
Note its 'scissor' tail.

Brown Booby (*Sula leucogaster*)   Plates 4 and 5

Global throughout the tropical oceans   *Range*

Most people who have visited the coasts of Great Britain   *Note*
will have seen that large white long-winged cigar-shaped
seabird with its black wing-tips which we call the Gannet.
Throughout the tropical zone seabirds of the same family
are known as 'Boobies'. In adult plumage Brown Boobies
are easily recognized by their wholly dark chocolate-brown
upperparts, head and neck contrasting sharply with the
white of the breast, belly and underside of the wings.
The young of all boobies vary considerably in colour with
brown mottling and it is not easy to distinguish one species
from another.
Boobies derive their name from their supposed stupidity.
The Red-footed Booby frequently flies on board ship, using

47

some part of the ship's structure as a vantage-point from which to dive in pursuit of flying-fish.

Plate 6   Common Noddies
             Crested Terns (*Sterna bergii*) and Sand Crabs

Range   The Crested Tern ranges throughout tropical and sub-tropical seas

Note   In full adult plumage the upperparts are pearly grey, and the forehead and underparts white. The crown and nape are black with the feathers elongated. The bill is greenish-yellow and the legs black.

A number of different varieties of Sand Crab, Land Crab, Coco-nut Crab and Hermit Crab abound in many tropical islands. There is ample evidence that some of these prey on the eggs and young of breeding terns and petrels.

Sand Crabs (*Ocypoda cursor*) have a shell width of only two inches and a total span of about one foot, including their long legs.

They have been seen hunting the burrows of petrels at night, dragging out young nestlings and tearing them to pieces. Reports vary, however, and on some islands the crabs seem harmless to the seafowl.

Plates 7 and 16   Common Noddies (*Anous stolidus*)

Range   Global throughout tropical and sub-tropical seas

The Common Noddy is the most widespread of the four species of noddies which inhabit the tropical zone. It is rather larger than the other three.

Note   Noddies belong to the same family as the graceful fork-tailed terns, but unlike the terns their tails have only a shallow wedge in the centre. Their nesting habits are different too, for, whilst terns nest on the ground, the noddies build flimsy structures of sticks and seaweed in the low trees and scrub. The Common Noddy is a uniformly dark brown bird, slightly paler below, with black primaries and tail, and with dark bill and legs. The dark colouring is relieved by an attractive lavender-grey crown.

In the photograph the right-hand bird may well be a White-capped Noddy.

| White Tern (*Gygis alba*) | Plates 10 to 12 |

Global throughout the tropical seas | *Range* |

Note

The beautiful White or 'Love' Tern is the most delicate of all the terns. Its bright blue needle-sharp bill, the black orbital ring round the dark eye, set high in the head, and its pale blue legs make a striking contrast to its pure white plumage.

White Terns seem to have little fear of humans and are easily approached. Where trees fringe the tropical island lagoons they will select a bare branch or fork on which to balance a single white egg. How these eggs remain in position during incubation is something of a mystery; certainly the bird will shuffle on and off her egg longitudinally along the branch. Needless to say, many young nestlings very soon tumble to the ground.

Blue-grey Noddies (*Procelsterna cerulea*) | Plate 13

Tropical Pacific Ocean | *Range*

Note

This noddy is confined to the Pacific Ocean and resorts to a great many islands in Oceania.

It is entirely blue-grey with black bill and legs.

Great Frigate-Bird (*Fregata minor*) | Plates 14 and 15

Tropical Indian and Pacific Oceans | *Range*

Note

Frigate-Birds or 'Man-o'-war Hawks' are the pirates and scavengers of the tropical islands.

Their black plumage, extraordinarily long narrow wings, slender yet cruel sharply hooked bills and black, deeply forked tails make them indeed unmistakable.

All day long they may be seen floating high in the air, circling on motionless wings, their tails opening and closing 'scissor' fashion, waiting to swoop on some unfortunate sea-bird and pursue it ruthlessly until it has disgorged its last meal. With a quick turn of the wings the Frigate will pounce on the titbit, usually before it reaches the sea.

During the breeding season they will 'work' colonies of nesting terns, flapping slowly over the nesting areas and snatching up chicks without pausing to settle, disposing of a youngster in two or three large gulps. Not infrequently they will find on return to their own nest that a neighbourly Frigate has seized the opportunity to gobble up their own egg.

Frigate-Birds construct large clumsy nests of sticks in the branches of trees or scrub, nesting in colonies, and laying one white egg.

The male has a bright-red distensible pouch at the throat, which it will blow up like a balloon as a nuptial display. Females have a greyish neck, merging into the white of the breast and sides.

The photograph shows the plumage of a female very clearly.

Plate 18   Wandering Albatross (*Diomedea exulans*)

Range   Throughout the southern oceans, chiefly between 60° south and 30° south but sometimes as far north as the Tropic of Capricorn

Note   With its immense wing-span of nine feet or more, its soft white adult plumage, gentle eye and fine pink bill, the Wandering Albatross is the most magnificent and the largest ocean bird.

Outside the breeding season 'Wanderers' remain in the open oceans, travelling vast distances in effortless planing flight, making full use of the continuous winds in these latitudes. They feed chiefly on squid and marine crustacea, but will pick up and follow ships all day long, never averse to any offal or scraps thrown overboard.

Seamen in sailing-ship days would bait triangles of metal and trail these astern. The greedy albatrosses gobbled the bait, whereupon the triangle stuck in their bills and they were hauled aboard to make pipe stems out of their hollow bones and baccy pouches out of the skin of their feet.

Wandering Albatrosses breed on the scattered islands around the southern oceans between 50° south and 60° south. They build mud castles usually amongst the clumps of tussock-grass and lay a single egg. The young bird remains nine months at the nest, and it is now almost certain that adults breed only every other year, returning at intervals to feed their young.

A Wandering Albatross can weigh as much as 25 lb.

Top
Great Skua
Stercorarius s. skua

Centre and bottom
Pintado Petrel
Daption capensis

B

Top right
Sooty Tern
  Sterna fuscata

Top left
Red-footed Booby
  Sula sula

Bottom
Blue-faced Booby
  Sula dactylatra

Ann Hughes
1961

C

Top right
Great Frigate-Bird ♀
Fregata minor

Top left
Brown Booby
Sula leucogaster

Bottom
Great Frigate-Bird ♂
Fregata minor

1961

D

Falkland Flightless Steamer (Loggerhead) Duck
Tachyeres brachypterus
Left ♀   Right ♂

White-capped Noddy (*Anous minutus*)   Plate 19

Tropical Atlantic and Pacific Oceans   *Range*

The White-capped Noddy differs from the Common   *Note*
Noddy only in being rather smaller in size, and having a
whiter cap. In the photograph, as the bird stands atop its
clumsily built nest, its white cap, long pointed bill, and
dark, almost black, plumage give it a striking appearance.

Wandering Albatross (*Diomedea exulans*)   Plates 20 and 22
Immature plumage

These photographs show very clearly the plumage of a   *Note*
young Wandering Albatross viewed from below.
Before leaving the nest the young birds appear first in a white
woolly coat of down. This they discard for an almost uniform brown plumage with the face white. On taking to the
ocean it is several years before they reach the full, almost
completely white, appearance save always for some dark
pencilling on the wing coverts and dark tips to wings
and tail.
In the phase shown the young bird will be almost uniformly
brown above, with the white undersurface of the wings and
the distinctive white head.
The bird in plate 22 has reached a later stage, where the
plumage on the mantle back and upper wings is mottled,
sometimes known as the leopard spot stage.

Wandering Albatross (*Diomedea exulans*)   Plate 21

The photograph shows the 'Wanderer' in full adult plumage   *Note*
making use of updraughts from the crests of the swell to
plane on motionless wings.

Black-browed Albatross or Mollymawk (*Diomedea*   Plate 23
    melanophris)

Southern oceans between about 60° south and the Tropic of   *Range*
Capricorn

The smaller albatrosses of the southern oceans are known to   *Note*
seamen as Mollymawks, but it must not be assumed that
they are like seagulls.

The Black-browed Mollymawk is about as big as a goose, and is rather like a huge Great Black-backed Gull. Its back and tail feathers are black and the upper surface of its wings a uniform brownish-black. Apart from the edges of its underwings the rest of the body, head and neck are white. It has a dark liquid eye, above which runs a dark streak of feathers, or black brow, giving it a gentle, grave expression. It is easily distinguished too by its bright yellow bill.

Like the 'Wanderers', the Black-browed Mollies nest amongst the tussock-grass on the slopes of the sub-Antarctic islands, sometimes, as in South Georgia, in enormous colonies of thousands of birds. Their nests of mud and tussock-grass have been described as standing for all the world like large cheddar cheeses in rows.

Like other albatrosses they indulge in elaborate nuptial displays. While the hen remains on the nest both bow courteously to each other, throw their heads backwards, braying loudly, then kiss and 'fence' with their beaks, when the male bird will spread wings and tail and execute a *pas de danse*.

Plate 24   Albatrosses and Petrels

    Note   In the harbours of South Georgia when the whale factories are working and the offal from the carcasses spreads over the water seabirds of every species congregate to enjoy the feast. Southern Black-backed Gulls line the jetties, Great Skuas put in an appearance while albatrosses, Giant Petrels, Cape Pigeons, Diving Petrels and prions squabble over the spoil. In the photograph two 'Wanderers' rise from the sea, while to the left a third, in full adult plumage, rides high on the water.

In the centre can be seen two brown-coloured Giant Petrels. A flock of Cape Pigeons occupy the foreground.

Plate 25   Rock-hopper Penguins (*Eudyptes crestatus*)

    Note   This delightful picture on Gough Island distinguishes the penguins from Macaroni Penguins largely by the white margins on both sides of the flipper.

Rock-hopper Penguins (*Eudyptes crestatus*). Adult and young   Plate 26

Southern oceans from sub-Antarctic islands northwards in   *Range*
winter to South America, South Africa, New Zealand
and southern Australia

The Rock-hopper is one of the medium-sized penguins,   *Note*
standing about two feet high, and derives its name from its
habit of proceeding on shore in a series of hops, keeping
both feet together.
Its back is bluish-grey with the upperside of the flippers a
darker slaty black, and its head, cheeks and chin are of this
same colour. It is easily distinguished in full adult plumage
by a line of pale yellow plumes running from behind the
nostrils to above the eye, the hinder plumes much elongated
and drooping. Its short stout bill is red or orange. Its flippers
have white margins.
The photograph was taken in the Falkland Islands where
they breed.
The young penguins have greyer cheeks and develop plumes
later.

Sooty Shearwaters (*Puffinus griseus*)   Plate 27

Southern Pacific and Atlantic Oceans from 60° south   *Range*
During the southern winter these shearwaters disperse
northwards, penetrating to the extreme North Pacific and
Atlantic, swinging southward once again as the southern
spring approaches.

The Sooty Shearwater, known as the 'Mutton Bird' in the   *Note*
New Zealand seas, is a medium-sized bird with blackish-
brown upperparts and greyish-brown underparts, the central
portion of the underwing being whitish. Its bill and feet are
dark. Sooty Shearwaters are sociable seabirds, sometimes
flocking in countless thousands at sea off New Zealand
waters. Like the Short-tailed Shearwater of the Bass Strait
(a very similar species), it has an economic value as a food
to the local inhabitants, who collect up the young birds.
Nowadays numbers taken up are strictly limited and the
local colonies are in no danger of extermination.
Sooties breed over a wide area from New Zealand to the
islands off Cape Horn and in the Falkland Islands.

Plates 28 to 31   Magellan Penguins (*Spheniscus magellanicus*)

Range   From the coasts of South America northwards to Chile and
Brazil and the Falkland Islands

Note   In the photographs these medium-sized penguins—they
stand about two feet six inches in height—are on a sandy
beach in the Falkland Islands where they breed.
The brownish-grey upperparts and white chest and underparts are set off by a smartly patterned face and neck, clearly
seen in plate 31.
In the Falkland Islands they are known locally as 'Jackass
Penguins' (really a different species) on account of their
braying call.
Penguins swim very low in the water, often with only their
necks showing above the surface. Plate 31 shows this attitude
clearly. Underwater they use their flippers only to propel
themselves at astonishing speed, their feet stretched out
behind them as steering oars. Sometimes they will travel by
a series of leaps and dives, and most species can leap from
below the surface to land on ice-shelves three to four feet
in height.
In plate 28 a single Gentoo Penguin stands in the centre taller
than the Jackasses and seems to be acting as traffic controller.

Plates 32 to 34   Falkland Flightless Steamer or Logger Duck (*Tachyeres
brachypterus*)

Range   Falkland Islands

Note   This curious flightless duck is confined to the Falkland
Islands, and though its eggs are collected every year for
human consumption, and it has no means of taking to the
air, it appears to be in no danger of extermination. Indeed
it is a quite common duck found on most inlets and beaches.
Loggers are essentially sea ducks, feeding in the sea below
the low-water mark, often diving for periods of over half a
minute, plucking at weed and searching amongst pebbles
and rocks for food.
The name 'Steamer' comes from its habit of steaming along
the surface at considerable speed, rocking from side to side
as it makes powerful thrusts with its feet. Loggers are also
capable of hauling themselves up vertical sea-walls, using
beak and nails.

By nature they are pugnacious and often engage in spectacular, if short-lived, fights, male attacking male, and female going for female. The sound of these combats can be heard far into the night. They do little damage to themselves.

When paired off, couples select particular lengths of beach territory and the ducks nest among the clumps of tussock-grass close to the beaches.

The birds seem to have no real enemies except perhaps the occasional seal. It is certain that when a seal bobs up amongst a flock of duck offshore, panic ensues and sends the flock dashing for the shore.

Prion (*Pachyptila species*)   Plate 38

Southern oceans from the Antarctic circle northwards to   *Range*
about 35° south

Commonly known to the old-time sealers and whalers as   *Note*
whale-birds, or ice-birds, these fragile little petrels are not much larger than Missel Thrushes. The six different species cannot be identified separately when viewed on the wing, differing only slightly in size, and in the shape and size of the bill.

The general colour of all these small prions is a delicate blue-grey above and white beneath, the white extending to the face. A dark streak through the eye, and darker coloration on the edge of the shoulders and along the scapulars and outer primaries forms an inverted W pattern when seen close to.

Prions often gather in immense flocks, presenting an unforgettable sight as they wheel simultaneously low over the sea, showing alternately flashes of grey upperparts and white underparts.

They feed on the myriads of small marine crustacea amongst the surface plankton, and can often be seen swimming on the surface with raised wings, occasionally diving, and scooping the food into the pouches at the base of their bills.

It is a marvel how these tiny birds can withstand the wildest gales and the bitter cold of the Antarctic latitudes.

Prions nest in burrows, perhaps two or three feet long, in the spongy earth, with a nesting chamber at the end containing one round white, and usually heavily stained, egg. Like most petrels they only return to their nesting burrows in the darkness and leave before dawn. Woe betide a laggard after daylight has flooded the hill-side. The Great Skuas will be on the alert to strike it down and tear it to pieces. Indeed the bleached bones of hundreds of prions are a common sight about the burrows.

Plates 39 to 44   Pintado Petrel or Cape Pigeon (*Daption capensis*)

Range   Global throughout the southern oceans from the Antarctic northwards to the Tropic of Capricorn

Note   Of all the petrels in the southern oceans the 'Cape Pigeon', as it is known to sailormen, is the most conspicuous. The dark brown and white skewball pattern of the upper wing surfaces, the brown head and chin and the pure white underparts make it unmistakable. It was named 'Pintado' —the painted bird—on account of its plumage. It is somewhat smaller than our common gull.

In the vicinity of the sub-Antarctic isles Cape Pigeons may often be seen in great numbers, frequenting the harbours of the whaling stations, feeding off the offal jettisoned from the few old-fashioned factories. While feeding they keep up an incessant babel of harsh throaty cries. In the open ocean they feed off the small marine life in the upper layers of the sea. Their habit of following in the wake of ships makes them well known to the seafarer.

Plates 45 to 50   Giant Petrel, Nelly or Stinker (*Macronectes giganteus*)

Range   Southern oceans northwards to Tropic of Capricorn

Note   As large as a small albatross, but altogether more stoutly built, the Giant Petrel is ugly in form and habits.

The more usual plumage is a dusky grey-brown with a much paler grey head and neck, and a pale greenish or straw-coloured bill. This is an enormous conk with a cruelly hooked tip. On top are the tubular nostrils and, like all petrels, the covering of the bill is divided into separate plates.

The small pale eye, like a jackdaw's, is shrouded by a ridge of feathers above, giving the bird an unpleasant frown.

Sailormen know the Giant Petrel as the Nelly or Stinker; anyone who has seen these ungainly birds scavenging over a seal's carcass or gobbling up young penguins will fully agree with them.

Giant Petrels breed in the same terrain as the albatrosses and mollymawks, usually in scattered colonies, making a pile of seaweed or tussock-grass and depositing one large white egg. When approached on the nest the inquisitive bird-watcher must beware, for the Stinker will not hesitate to spew its last meal straight towards him to a distance of two or three yards —the Stinker!

| Sheathbill (*Chionis alba*) | Plates 51 and 52 |
| Antarctic Islands | *Range* |

The sheathbills are something of a paradox. Viewed casually *Note* they look very much like white pigeons, and they are one of the few birds of the Antarctic islands whose feet are not webbed.

The Norwegians call them by the Norsk name for ptarmi-gan, 'Rype', but they are nearer to the plovers, yet if they land in the sea they can swim! When they fly, with their short rounded wings, they flap along awkwardly enough, but they may often be found many miles from land, settling on rafts of kelp or on ice-floes.

They are not active birds onshore and are unpleasant feeders, stealing eggs and eating seal excrement and all manner of filth. They are, on the other hand, good eating. The sheathbill's most unusual feature is its beak. The base of the upper beak is covered with a heavy sheath like a second bill from which the bird gets its name, and above this sheath and stretching below the eye there is a curious pinkish crinkled wattle, giving it a 'scabby' look.

| Adélie Penguins (*Pygoscelis adeliae*) | Plates 64 and 65 |
| Antarctic Seas | *Range* |

This charming and inquisitive little penguin claims with *Note* the Emperor Penguin the honour of breeding on the Ant-arctic continent itself. The photographs show the smart black-and-white plumage, the white eyelids and the long pointed tail. What the pictures do not show, however, is the brick-red bill and rosy white upper sides of the feet.

The bird in the foreground of plate 64 is tucking its egg away before settling on it. Adélies incubate by lying on their eggs and the dirty fronts to their underparts arise from this cause.

Adélies stand upright, walking with a waddling gait, but when travelling over the snow they will travel on their breasts, propelling themselves with their flippers.

Plate 66   Gentoo Penguins (*Pygoscelis papua*)

Range   Southern oceans from Antarctica northwards, breeding on most islands in the southern oceans

Note   This penguin is easily distinguished by the white band it carries across the back of its head from eye to eye. It has a rather long tail and white edgings to both sides of its flippers. Its attractive orange feet and bill makes 'Johnny', for this is its common name to the seafarer, a smart fellow indeed.

At their breeding rookeries they are aggressive and will peck viciously at an intruder.

Plate 67   King Penguins (*Aptenodytes patagonica*) with two Gentoo Penguins (*Pygoscelis papua*) in the foreground

Note   This fine photograph captures a group of King Penguins in a typical setting on the beach at South Georgia with a back-ground of tussock-grass. It is on this terrain that the penguins breed.

In front stand two Gentoo Penguins, smaller in stature by almost a foot and easily distinguished by the white band across the back of the head, stretching from eye to eye, and by the white margins to their flippers.

Plate 68   King Penguin Rookery

Note   Penguins are sociable birds and gather in great rookeries, sometimes of many thousands, to court and breed. The noise on these rookeries is deafening, the birds keeping up incessant throaty cries, with much lowering and raising of bills. When the birds first arrive from sea it seems doubtful if they can differentiate between the sexes. Males will bring

E

Top
Giant Petrel
Macronectes giganteus

Centre
White-chinned Petrel
Procellaria aequinoctialis

Bottom
Short-tailed Shearwater
Puffinus tenuirostris

Ann Hughes
1961

F

1. Rockhopper Penguin
    Eudyptes crestatus

2. Macaroni Penguin
    Eudyptes chrysolophus

3. Chinstrap (Bearded) Penguin
    Pygoscelis antarctica

4. King Penguin
    Aptenodytes patagonica

5. Emperor Penguin
    Aptenodytes forsteri

6. Gentoo Penguin
    Pygoscelis papua

7. Adélie Penguin
    Pygoscelis adeliae

8. Magellan Penguin
    Spheniscus magellanic

Top
White Tern
Gygis alba

Centre
Common Noddy
Anous stolidus

Bottom
Crested Tern
Sterna bergii

Ann Hughes
1961

H

Ann Hughes
1961

pebbles in their bills and bowing low deposit them before other males, who remain indifferent to such blandishments. Finally the sexes pair off.

In the foreground of the photograph are two down-covered youngsters, whilst in some adults the pouch of skin is seen to be lowered over the feet.

Young King Penguins in down   Plate 69

Young penguins are covered in down when first hatched, *Note* and they retain this until shortly before moulting and donning their quill feathers and taking to the sea.

In the latter stages of down they look larger than their parents, and it is a ludicrous sight to watch them thrusting their heads into the gullets of their parents for a meal of half-digested marine food.

King Penguin (*Aptenodytes patagonica*)   Plates 70 and 71

Southern oceans from Cape Horn eastwards amongst the *Range* sub-Antarctic isles

Standing over three feet in height, the King Penguin is the *Note* second largest of the penguin family, eclipsed only by the Emperor Penguin.

No black-and-white photograph can convey the boldness of its colourful, nay royal, robes. The back and upper sides of the flippers are bluish-grey margined by a narrow black line on each side of the white breast and underparts. The velvet black head is offset by bright orange patches on each side, connecting with an orange-yellow collar, whilst the black bill is slashed by a red flash along the base of the lower mandible. Walking and running with a perfectly upright carriage, it would by any standard be judged the king of the penguins. The female does not stoop to incubate its single egg, but remains erect, holding the egg in a fold of skin between its legs.

King Penguins   Plate 72

The sea is their true element, and it is here that all their food *Note* is obtained: crustacea, fish or cuttlefish. They have only one real enemy in this element, the Leopard Seal.

Index

Index

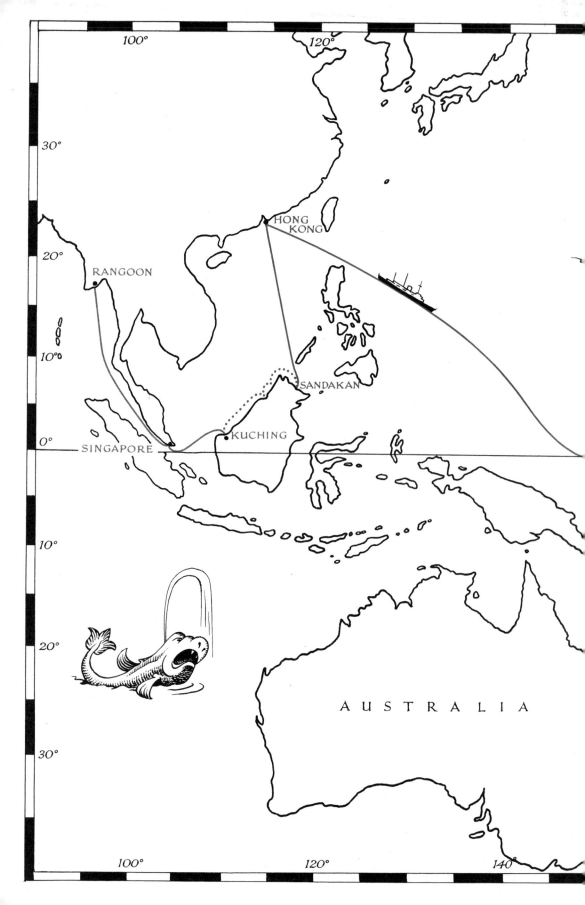